Love Your Cockatiel

Love Your Cockatiel

Roy Stringer

W. Foulsham & Co. Ltd.
London • New York • Toronto • Cape Town • Sydney

PUBLISHED for Petcetera Press,
235 West First Street,
Bayonne, N.J. 07002. by
W. Foulsham & Company Limited
Yeovil Road, Slough, Berkshire, SL1 4JH

ISBN 0-572-01386-8

Printed in Spain by Cayfosa, Barcelona.
Dep. Leg. B-27227-1986

Photographs — pages 2, 19, 23, 43, 53, 60 & 61 by Mrs
Dulcie Cooke. All other photographs by Colin O'hara.

Page 2:   Pearl Pied Cock

Contents

1 **The Decision to Keep a Cockatiel**

So you think that you would like to keep a cockatiel? Have you thought what this involves? Keeping a pet of any kind is a responsibility. A cockatiel must be fed and watered every day and cleaned out at least once a week. If you go away on holiday someone must be found to do these jobs for you. A cockatiel needs a good cage and this will cost money; so will the equipment such as drinkers and feeders.

But keeping a cockatiel will give you a lot of pleasure. They tame easily, learn to talk and come to know their owners. It has been said that the cockatiel is a bird which has every virtue and not a single fault. If you decide to keep several cockatiels you will be able to breed from them and it can turn into an interesting hobby. If you go to bird shows you will be able to meet other cockatiel breeders and widen your knowledge of these lovely birds.

2 **Housing**

Whether you are going to buy a pet cockatiel, or more than one for breeding, it is best to have a cage ready for when you arrive home. This will mean that the bird will be put into its own home and not be disturbed by being kept in some temporary housing.

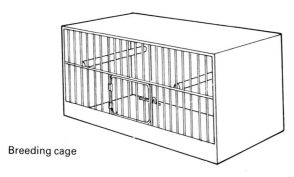

Breeding cage

If you are going to keep a pet cockatiel in the house there are lots of designs of cage available in pet shops. Many of them will house your cockatiel safely and comfortably as long as they are large enough. You must remember that cockatiels are quite large at about 32 cm long (12½ in). There must be enough room for your pet to spread its wings as well as allowing for its height. Your pet shop owner will be able to advise you. Cages made for parrots are ideal for cockatiels. Those with plastic bottoms which can be removed for cleaning and disinfecting are better than the ones with metal bottoms which can become rusty.

Some pet cages have perches which are too small in diameter. Perches should be no smaller than 15mm (5/8 in) diameter. Having different sizes, say one of 15mm and another of 20mm (3/4 in), is best. But perches are easily changed, so if you find a cage which suits you do not be put off by the perches. Change them.

If you want to cage-breed cockatiels you will need a large cage. Flights are better. A cage can be made quite cheaply from plywood and a wire cage front bought from a pet shop. It must be at least 1.5m long (5ft). Once more, the length of a fully-grown cockatiel must be taken into account so a height of 90cm (3ft) is called for and a depth of 60cm (2 ft).

Even more attention needs to be paid to perches in breeding cages. Cockatiels mate on the perch and if a perch is not fixed firmly it can be the cause of infertile eggs. The hen needs to be able to grip the perch during mating and so at least one of them should be square in section. A length of wood, 15mm (1/2in) square, with the sharp corners removed, serves very well.

If you have a garden an aviary is an ideal place to house and breed cockatiels. The size of the aviary will depend on the size of your garden and how many birds you intend to keep. A wooden frame 1.8m × 1.8m × 1.8m (6ft × 6ft × 6ft) covered with 12 mm (1/2in) wire netting will comfortably house three pairs of cockatiels. Welded wire mesh, 25mm × 12mm (1in × 1/2in) is a good alternative to the netting. 19 gauge (thickness) is thick enough but 16

Corrugated plastic Shelter

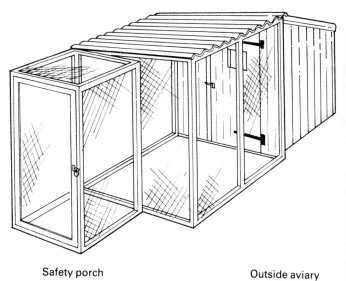

Safety porch

Outside aviary

gauge is better. Always fix the wire to the inside of the wooden frame.

The birds will also need a waterproof and draughtproof shelter to sleep in. This can form one end of the flight and, for the size of aviary described, a depth of 90cm (3ft) would be large enough. The shelter should have a large door into the flight, which can be opened in hot weather and for cleaning out. A small door – 15cm (6in) square – can be used for the birds to get from the shelter to the flight. Both doors can be closed when the birds have gone in to roost for the night. The shelter must be fitted with plenty of perches so that every bird can find a place it likes. In the flight, small branches from fruit trees can be used as perching. Do not use the wood from other trees.

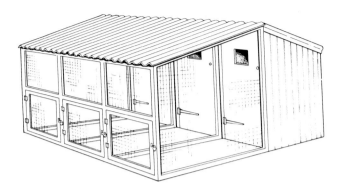

Several small flights can be built as a block for controlled breeding

You will need to take care when building the door from your garden into the flight, which you will need to use when you go in to feed, clean out or even just stand admiring your birds. You must make sure that the birds do not fly past you and escape as you are going in. The first rule is that flight doors should always open inwards so that you fill the door opening as you go in. Safest of all is a small wire-mesh covered porch. With this, you open a door, step into the porch, close the first door and then open the door into the flight. If you do not have a porch, then a door only about 1m (3ft 3in) high can be used. You will find that as you enter the cockatiels will fly up and away and this will give you time to go in without any escaping.

The roof of the flight should be covered with sheets of corrugated plastic. This will keep out the droppings of wild birds – which could carry disease – and help to protect your cockatiels from cats. Garden soil and lawn are not suitable floors for flights. They soon become messy and are very difficult to clean. Best are either concrete or a thick layer of gravel which can be washed with a hose pipe.

If you wish to control-breed in flights then each pair will require a flight half the size of the aviary described; 1.8m × 1.8m × 1.8m (6ft × 6ft × 6ft). The shelter must also be divided. Standard aviary panels, 2m × 1m (6ft × 3ft) can be bought quite cheaply from many pet shops and by fitting these together a whole range of flights can be built and added to.

3 Equipment

The equipment you need for your cage consists mainly of feeding utensils. You can use dishes and bowls not made specially for cockatiels but it is better to use feeders and drinkers which have been specially designed.

If you give water in an open dish it will soon become full of seed husks and droppings, and will not be clean enough for your cockatiel to drink. Your pet will also play in the water at a time when you do not want him to get wet. You also have to open the door to put the water dish into the cage. The best utensil for giving water is a plastic water fountain of the larger type used for seed with smaller birds. This clips on to the outside of the cage, will not fill up with seed husks or droppings and can be changed without opening the cage door. The part of the fountain inside the cage is too small for your cockatiel to be able to bathe when you do not want him to. The open dish, already in the pet cage when you buy it, can be used for grit.

The same type of water fountain can be used on a breeding cage, but if you keep several pairs in a flight you need something which will hold more water. You can buy a galvanised base which holds a plastic lemonade bottle. This is a standard animal drinker.

An open dish is better for seed than water but still has the problem that droppings can get in with the seed. There are many types of seed-hopper on the market but you must be careful of which type to use with cockatiels. This is because their favourite seed mixture contains sunflower seeds and these are large enough to block some hoppers. Ask the advice of your pet shop owner.

It is best also to buy a clip to hold a piece of cuttlefish bone. This stops the bone getting dirty by lying around on the cage floor.

Some cockatiels love to take a bath. A shallow dish of water will give them the opportunity but it must be removed as soon as the water becomes dirty. It is better for birds to bath early in the day so that they have time to dry their feathers before roost to go to sleep for the night.

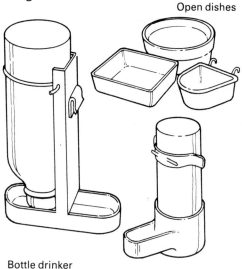

Open dishes

Bottle drinker

Plastic water fountain

Pied

4 **Selecting the Variety**

When deciding which variety of cockatiel to buy it is really a matter of which colour you like. Unlike some other animals and birds, all varieties of cockatiel are more or less the same size. If you see a cockatiel which is larger than others it will be because it has been bred by someone who shows his birds and has chosen big birds to breed from.

The first cockatiels to be domesticated were Grey cockatiels, sometimes referred to as Normals. Since then several new varieties have appeared by chance and skilled breeders have bred more of the same colour. Among the new colours are Lutinos, Pieds, Cinnamons (sometimes called Fawns or Isabelles), Pearled and Silvers. Some of these can be combined together to further increase the range. So we have Cinnamon Pied, Cinnamon Pearled, Pearled Pied and Cinnamon Pearled Pied cockatiels available.

When choosing a cockatiel as a pet there are far more important things to consider than the variety, these are explained in Chapter 5. There is no truth in the story that some varieties of cockatiel are easier to teach to talk than others. It is all a matter of which colour and markings you like best, although you will have to pay more for rarer coloured birds. You

Normal

will see a range of varieties in pet shops and at bird shows.

The following information will help you to identify some of the varieties of cockatiel: Normal cockatiel cocks are mainly grey. There is a bright patch of orange over the ears which is partly bordered by a narrow strip of white. The rest of the head and crest is yellow. The crest is tipped with grey. A broad band of white can be seen on the edge of the wing. The rest of the plumage is grey except for the underside of the tail which is black. The beak and legs are grey as is the cere – the fleshy area above the beak. Normal cockatiel hens are not usually as darkly coloured as cocks and the orange ear patches and the yellow of the head are paler. Some females have crests which are entirely grey. The underside of the hen's tail is barred with grey and yellow.

Young birds resemble the hen but have short tails and pinkish ceres. They are difficult to sex until they get their adult plumage although experts can detect a difference in song at an early age. Another aid to sexing is that young birds and hens have light mottling on the underside of the main wing flight feathers. Adult cock birds do not have these marks.

Pieds

Pieds have the same colouring as Normal Greys but the colour is interrupted by patches of white or primrose yellow. There is no pattern in the markings and some Pieds carry much more white than others. If the white covers areas used to tell which sex a bird is – such as the underside of the tail – sexing can

Cinnamon Pearl Pieds

be difficult. Then the distinctive warbling whistle of the cock may be the best indication.

Cinnamons

In all birds the Cinnamon factor brings softer tones and brown where there are normally black markings. So the grey of Normal cockatiels is overlaid with a warm brown tint. The yellow areas are soft in tone and the ear patches, orange red. Cinnamons have pinkish legs and plum-coloured eyes. The distribution of colour in both cocks and hens is the same as that of Normals.

Pearled

The basic colouring of Pearled cockatiels is the same as the Normal Grey. What brings the extra touch of beauty is that the back and wings are covered with white or yellow pearly markings. Cock birds revert to normal when about six months to a year old but hens keep their beautiful pearling.

Lutinos

Lutino cockatiels are basically white in colour with different shades of yellow in the places which are yellow on Normals. Their orange-red ear patches are even more noticeable because of the pale background. The legs are pinkish and eyes dark red. Hens can be identified easily as signs of the yellow bars on the underside of the tail remain.

Pearled Lutino

Silvers

Silver cockatiels are very rare. Their markings are distributed as in the Normal but instead of Grey the basic colouring is metallic silver.

Cinnamon Pieds

These have the distribution of markings of Pieds and the colouring of Cinnamons.

Cinnamon Pearled

These have the distribution of markings of Pearled and the colouring of Cinnamons.

Pearled Pieds

These have the same markings and colouring of Pearled cockatiels, overlaid with irregular light patches of Pieds.

Cinnamon Pearled Pieds

These are like Pearled Pieds but have the colouring of Cinnamons.

A Pair of Lutinos

5 Buying a Cockatiel

Before going out to buy a cockatiel, you should make up your mind where your interest lies. Do you want a friendly pet, which will learn to talk? Or do you want to breed these crested beauties?

If it is a pet you want, you must buy a young cock bird which is still in its baby feathering. Hens will learn to talk, but cocks are much easier to teach. If you buy from a pet shop the owner can help you in choosing the best bird. If you buy from an established breeder of cockatiels he or she will most likely know which chicks are cocks or hens. If a mistake is made, many breeders will be willing to exchange your chick for another. They usually prefer to keep more hens than cocks.

What to look for when buying a pet cockatiel

When you think you have found the cockatiel you would like as a pet, take a good look at it and check out several things.

1. Is the bird a young cock?
   You will most likely need help here, but, if there is a choice of several youngsters, choose the one which has the brightest yellow and orange colouring.

2. Is it healthy?
   A bird which looks happy and bright, moving about busily, is a fit bird. A wide-open bright eye is another good sign. Any bird which sits quietly, with its eyes partly closed and feathers fluffed up, should not be bought.
3. Are the nostrils clean and dry?
   Wet nostrils can show that a cockatiel is unwell.
4. Are the feathers under the vent clean?
   If a bird has dirty vent feathers it may have a stomach upset. It is best left and another bird chosen.

What to look for when buying cockatiels to breed

If you are buying cockatiels to breed from, it is best to choose cocks and hens which are about twelve months old and have never been used for breeding. If you buy from a breeder who shows his birds, his breeding records will show each bird's age. All of the health checks when buying a pet cockatiel (above) also apply to breeding birds. You should also check:

a) Is the bird the sex you want?
   The descriptions of the colours given in Chapter 4 should enable you to check the sex of most cockatiels you are offered. The bars on the underside of a hen's tail are one of the most easily seen signs.
b) Is a hen able to lay eggs?
   Fat hens often have difficulty when laying eggs so they should be avoided.

c) Are there any toes missing?
Any cockatiel with toes missing can have difficulty when gripping a perch. This is particularly important in hens as it can result in incomplete mating and infertile eggs. This is a minor point, but when buying breeding stock it is advisable to avoid as many faults as possible.

6 **Food and Water**

Seed

The basic food a cockatiel needs is a mixture of plain canary seed, millets, sunflower seeds, oats and a small quantity of hemp seed. The seeds come from all over the world and this helps to make sure that there is everything in the seed to make a cockatiel strong and fit. When you look at mixed seed, you will see a brown seed which is pointed at both ends. This is canary seed and should make up about half of the mixture. Millets are usually round in shape and come in various colours and sizes. Pearl white millet is large and white. Panicum millet is small and yellow. Japanese millet is brown and Dakota millet is red. These, with a few whole clipped oats, should make up about a quarter of the main mixture. A mixture of various types and sizes of sunflower seeds should make up the last quarter. Only a little hemp should be added as, although most cockatiels love hemp, it makes them fat if they eat too much.

Some pet shops have ready-made seed mixtures suitable for cockatiels. Usually the more you buy at one time, the less it will cost to feed your birds. When your birds are breeding it is best to increase the amount of plain canary seed in the mixture. A cockatiel needs to have seed available at all times.

Water

A cockatiel needs to have clean drinking water available at all times. From time to time you can add a vitamin additive or tonic to the drinking water. These can be bought from good pet shops. When adding anything to your cockatiels' water always read the instructions carefully and do not add more than the stated amount. Cockatiels require only small amounts of additives.

Grit

Cockatiels need a supply of grit so that they can digest their food. When they eat seeds, they remove the husk and swallow the kernel whole. A store of grit, kept in the crop, grinds up the seeds before they pass further into the digestive system. Grit comes in the form of Mineral, Limestone and Oystershell grits. All work equally well. It is thought that grit which is too sharp can damage the inside of a cockatiel's crop and so it is best to buy a good brand which has been specially prepared for parrot-like birds the size of cockatiels.

Cuttlefish Bone

Cockatiels like to chew at a piece of cuttlefish bone. They benefit from the calcium they consume as this helps to make their bones strong. Breeding hens need calcium to form the shells of the eggs they lay.

Iodine Block

Iodine blocks can be bought from pet shops, ready to fix on to the wires of the cage. By

chewing the block your cockatiel will benefit from iodine and minerals which will help to keep it healthy.

Greenfood

Cockatiels love to eat greenfood but you must be very careful when feeding it. The cheapest form of greenfood is dandelion leaves and chickweed but there is a risk involved when using these. If wild greens have been sprayed, to kill weeds or insects, they can be dangerous to feed to your cockatiel. There is also a risk that a dog or cat has used the ground around the weeds as a toilet. Any greens should be washed and dried before feeding to your birds. So it is best to feed greens which you grow yourself or buy at a greengrocers. Lettuce, spinach and cress are suitable.

Greens should be fed early in the day and in small quantities. They are absorbed quickly into the digestive system and if fed in the evening can lead to a bird spending the night with an empty crop. The remains of greens should be removed from the cage the same day that they are given to avoid the eating of stale food. Greens can be fed two or three times a week.

Treats

As well as their basic diet cockatiels love to sample all sorts of food. Perhaps the best known is the Millet Spray. Millet Sprays should be looked upon as a treat as cockatiels can get on very well without them, but some would eat nothing else if given the chance. A

Cinnamon Pearl

spray can be very useful to give to a cockatiel which looks a little off colour, but if eaten all the time can make a bird fat.

Small slices of carrot or fresh fruit, such as sweet apple are good for cockatiels. Any left over should be removed from the cage the same day. Although some cockatiels will eat almost anything, there are foods which are best avoided if your bird is not to get too fat. Such foods are bread, cake and biscuits. The exception to this is when feeding pairs which themselves are feeding chicks. Then, bread and milk is an ideal food. To sum up: a cockatiel must have seed, water and grit available all of the time. Care should be taken when feeding extra food as this can make your cockatiel fat. A fat bird is not a fit bird.

7 General Management and Training

The management of a cockatiel – or several cockatiels – is very simple. It need take only a few minutes each day, with an extra effort once a week when cleaning out. This means that, when you buy a cockatiel, you will be able to look after it properly and still have plenty of time to enjoy its company.

You need to find a good position for your cockatiel's cage. A cool, airy place is best, so avoid draughts and direct sunshine. This means that placing a cage in a window is *not* a good idea. Being placed in a draught can cause your cockatiel to become ill.

The position of seed and water feeders is also important. Seed and water must never be placed in position where your bird's droppings can get into them. Under a perch is the *worst* possible place. The same is true of any other item you put into the cage such as cuttlefish bone, millet sprays, greens and fruit. Find a position where they will stay clean.

Both seed and water need your attention every day. The water container should be washed and then rinsed thoroughly, before being refilled with fresh water. When a hopper is used it should be checked every day to see that there is plenty of seed inside and that the seed outlets are not blocked. Seed husks are not usually a problem with this type of feeder.

If it looks as though the level of seed has not gone down, check at once. This can mean that there is a blockage and that your cockatiel cannot get at its seed.

When seed is fed in an open dish the empty seed husks tend to lie on top. These need to be blown off every day, taking care not to get a seed husk in your eye. When the seed husks are gone you will be able to see how much seed is left in the dish. Even then, check once more as sometimes you will find a layer of dust in the bottom of the dish. Fill up the seed dish every day. A pet cockatiel will sleep better if you place a piece of light cloth over its cage late in the evening.

Training

Cockatiels kept in breeding cages and flights do not need training. But a lot of the pleasure of keeping a pet cockatiel is seeing how easy it is to train.

First you need to gain the pet's confidence and, although you may find it difficult, you must leave the bird alone for the first day after you have put it into the cage. This will give it time to settle down after all of the upset of being moved. It may sit quietly at first but as it becomes more sure of itself it will investigate the cage and start to chirp. When you go to the cage say the same two words, quietly, over and over again. If you are good at training, these will be the first two words your pet will say. "Hallo", followed by its name, or "Pretty Boy" are good starter words.

When you are sure that your pet is not afraid of you, gently open the cage door and slowly

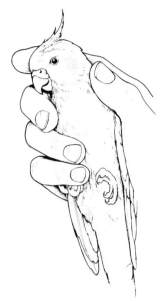
Holding a Cockatiel

put your hand into the cage. If the bird panics, slowly remove your hand, close the door and wait until it settles down before trying again. When the bird accepts your hand in its cage, extend your first finger and place it gently against its chest. You may find that your cockatiel will step on to your finger at this point.

If it does not, then press your finger gently against the bird's chest. This almost always causes it to step on to your finger. Still moving very slowly, gently transfer your pet on to another perch. It will soon get used to this and know what to expect when you next do it.

When your cockatiel has learned this lesson well, you can try bringing it out of the cage. But before doing so there are several things to

check to make sure that it will be safe. Make sure that all doors and windows are closed. If you have an open fireplace, make sure that it is guarded. Pull the curtain across any clear glass windows, or your pet, not knowing that there is any glass there, will fly into it and may damage itself. If you have a cat or dog make sure that they are not in the room. When your bird flies around the room watch what it is doing as cockatiels will chew house plants if left to do so. This can make them ill. If your cockatiel has learned its lesson well, you should have no difficulty getting it back into its cage. Just follow the method used when training to get it onto your finger and put your hand back into the cage. If it forgets its training and refuses to come to your hand you have more of a problem. First darken the room, which will permit you to get close, without your pet flying off. Then throw a soft cloth over it to capture it.

Cockatiels are very gentle birds but many of them object to being handled. In case they bite, it is as well to wear a thick glove such as is used for gardening. Best of all, handle cockatiels as little as possible. You must be firm enough to prevent the bird hurting itself, but not so firm as to hurt it yourself. By placing your thumb on one side of the cockatiels face, your forefinger on the back of its head and your second finger on the other side of its face, with the wings and body in the palm of your hand, you will be holding the bird safely. Then return it to the cage. Carry on training your pet to stand on your finger until you can return it to the cage without capturing it.

When your cockatiel is standing on your finger see if it will let you gently stroke the back of its head. If it does, your training is going well. You can also offer titbits of its favourite food to be taken from your finger. Always move slowly and gently as if you frighten your pet it will take much longer for it to become tame.

Repeating the same two word phrase over and over again, to reassure your cockatiel, will have made a start to teaching it to talk. Do not change the words until it has learned to say the first two. The more often you repeat the words the quicker your pet will learn them. Once it has learned the first words you can start teaching another two. If you are a good teacher it will not be long before your cockatiel knows lots of words.

8 Cleaning Out

Any pet needs to be cleaned out regularly. It depends on you to keep its housing and equipment clean. Cockatiels need to be cleaned out at least once a week. You can buy sand paper sheets from a pet shop which make cleaning out very simple, as far as the floor of the cage is concerned. It is just a matter of removing the old sheet and putting a new sheet in its place. Cockatiels often chew these sand sheets. This does them no harm.

It is a little cheaper to use bird sand on the floor of a cage, but it will take a little more time to remove the sand and to replace it. In breeding cages, wood shavings are often used to cover the cage floor. These are not so good in pet cages as they tend to come out of the cage when the cockatiel flutters its wings. If you do decide to use wood shavings, buy them from a pet shop. Shavings bought from a wood yard may have been treated with chemicals which could make your bird ill. The cheapest of all cage floor coverings is a piece of newspaper. This works well but does not look as attractive as the others.

About once a month you should disinfect the cage and equipment. Use a mild disinfectant and rinse feeders and water containers well in clean water before refilling them. Disin-

A pair of Pearled Pied

fectant should be used more often if a cockatiel has a stomach upset and its droppings are green instead of the normal black and white. Perches need special attention when cleaning out. They can become very dirty with the bird's droppings which, if left, get hard and could damage a cockatiel's feet. Perches should be scrubbed with disinfectant, rinsed and dried before being put back in the cage.

Cockatiel young being hand reared with a spoon

9 **Health**

Cockatiels are hardy birds which can stand a wide range of conditions without becoming ill. Some item of food, causing a stomach upset, or being placed in a draught, bringing on a cold, are the most usual causes of illness. They are naturally bright, active birds and so the first sign of illness can be that they sleep longer than is usual. A small change to the diet or position of the cage at this stage can stop the illness going any further. But if your cockatiel reaches the stage where it is huddled up on the floor of the cage it is time to get the advice of a vet, preferably one who has experience of birds.

Enteritis

Stomach upsets are the most common form of illness in birds. The appearance of the bird and its droppings are both signs that a cockatiel is suffering from enteritis. A slight case will see a cockatiel sitting quietly, feathers fluffed up rather than smooth, sleeping more than usual with its head under its wing and its droppings will be green rather than the normal black and white. In a severe case the fluffing up will be to the point where the bird's head seems to be withdrawn into its body and its eyes will be closed. The bird's droppings will be coating its vent and tail. The first steps in treating any case of stomach upset is to move the bird to a warm place and remove any food other than the seed mixture. Green food is often the cause of enteritis, particularly if it is stale, dirty, wet or has been subject to frost. So make sure that your bird eats no green food while it is ill. Even when your bird is well all green food should be taken from the cage at the end of each day so that it cannot be eaten when it is stale.

Pet shops sell medicines which can be put in a cockatiel's drinking water. In slight cases of stomach upsets, one of these can be tried for a couple of days. If the bird gets no better then you should consult a vet. In serious cases it is best to speak to a vet straight away.

Sickness

Sickness, like enteritis is caused by a stomach upset but results in a bird bringing up the contents of its stomach through the beak. This clings, in a sticky mess, to the face and head of a cockatiel. Because it is a stomach upset, treatment begins as it did for enteritis.

Keep the bird warm and take away all food except the seed. Make sure that the bird has no green food to eat. Try a medicine, from a pet shop, at first, but if the bird is no better after a couple of days consult a vet. If, at any stage, the bird becomes more ill, speak to a vet at once.

When a bird is sick, the food it brings up is wet and sometimes has an unpleasant smell.

Moult

Moulting cannot be called an illness as it is just a case of a bird dropping its old feathers so that it can grow new ones. In the wild this happens once a year, but the changes of temperature, in a house, can cause it to happen more often. A bird which is moulting is more liable to become ill and so it should be kept in a temperature as constant as possible. A tonic in the drinking water helps a cockatiel when it is moulting.

Feather Plucking

There are two types of feather plucking. The plucking of other birds' feathers – usually a mother pulling the feathers out of her chicks – and cases of a cockatiel plucking its own feathers. Hens in nest boxes sometimes start pulling out feathers from their chicks' heads. What starts as a show of affection can become more serious when a hen wants the chicks to leave the nest so that she can lay another clutch of eggs. A cream can be bought, to be rubbed on the chicks' heads, which helps to stop the hen plucking. Feathers plucked from the head usually grow back in. Hens which feather pluck should not be used for breeding again; nor should the young hens bred from them. Many people think that feather plucking is an inherited habit.

When a bird starts to pull out its own feathers it is almost certainly due to one of two causes; a feather mite or stress. No matter what the cause it pays to treat for mite. Pet shops sell powders and sprays which can be used both on birds and equipment. If the cause is a mite it can be cured quickly in this way.

Stress is more difficult. If a cockatiel becomes so bored that it sits and pulls out its own feathers you must find a way of keeping it occupied. Changing the position of the cage can help, even to the point of moving it to another room where the bird will get more company. When a cockatiel is left alone during the day, leave the radio playing quietly to keep it company. As a last resort, buy a second cockatiel, but it is just possible that they will not get on together and there is a good chance that the arrival of another bird will stop your pet from talking.

Claws

Sometimes a cockatiel's claws can become overgrown. Some pet shops sell perches with sandpaper fixed to the underside. These can help to keep claws the correct length.

The cutting of claws is best left to experts. At the centre of claws are blood vessels and cutting by an inexperienced person can cause bleeding to occur. If you do cut a claw, check where the blood vessel stops – by holding up to the light – and cut no closer than 3mm (⅛in) to this. If you should cut and cause bleeding dip the claw in an antiseptic solution and all should be well within a few hours. if it is not then consult a vet.

Egg Binding

Occasionally, when breeding, a cockatiel hen

becomes egg bound. All hens become swollen under the vent when they are laying and this should not be confused with egg binding. If a hen looks bright and alert it is *not* egg bound. An egg bound hen looks fluffed up and unwell; often sitting on the floor of the cage. Keeping the hen warm is often all that is required for it to pass the egg. A little olive oil brushed on to the vent opening helps. As a last resort the hen can be held over a cup of hot water so that the steam can relax the vent. Be very careful not to let the hen be scalded. If possible, the advice of an experienced breeder of cockatiels should be sought.

Injuries

Injuries, such as broken legs and wings, should be treated as quickly as possible by a vet.

General

Never be afraid to ask the advice of an experienced breeder if you are worried that your cockatiel might be ill. When giving medicine in the drinking water always make sure that the dose is that stated on the bottle and take away any other drinking water.

10 **Breeding**

Cockatiels will breed at any time of the year if they are fit and given the correct conditions. This is because in the wild they are triggered to breed, not by the season of the year, but by water being available. Even in the deserts of Australia, rain means that grasses will begin to grow. By going to nest when it rains, cockatiels know that there will be food for their chicks by the time they hatch.

If you wish to breed with your cockatiels in winter it must be indoors and you should be prepared to provide artificial lighting so that there are at least 12 hours in which parents can feed their chicks. Heating is not required as long as the temperature in the room, where the breeding cage is housed, remains above 7°C (45°F). However, breeding cockatiels is best left until spring brings warmer weather and longer days.

All you need to do to start your cockatiels breeding – assuming they are fit – is to give them a nest box. There are breeders who can succesfully breed cockatiels on a colony system – several pairs in the same flight. However the best chance of success comes with one pair to each enclosure. In addition, colony breeding permits any cock to pair with any hen which is not always desirable when birds are related to each other.

If you particularly want to try colony breeding there are guidelines which are best to follow. Do not overcrowd the enclosure; make sure that there are equal numbers of cocks and hens; put in more nest boxes than there are pairs – to give the hens a choice; fix all nest boxes high in the flight, all level with each other. Even if you do all these things you are likely to meet problems. People who breed cockatiels in colonies spend a lot of time watching to see that all of the birds get on well together. Any bird which does not fit in is replaced with another until a compatible collection is established. Without doubt the easiest way of breeding cockatiels is to have one pair to each flight.

Cockatiels will nest happily in a wooden box 38cm high by 25cm square (15in × 10in × 10in). They will not mind if the box is a little larger and design detail is not important. In the bottom of the box it is best to have a thick layer of material on which the hen can lay her eggs. Suitable materials are peat and coarse sawdust. Some breeders provide a mixture of the two. The peat remains moist which helps the eggs to hatch. The box will need a hole cut in it, about 6cm (2½in) in diameter so that the pair can get in and out. A perch, just below the hole, is appreciated as is a ladder of wood or wire mesh fixed on the inside. The last thing that is needed is a door for you to be able to look in, to check that everything is going well. When breeding in cages, nest boxes are best mounted on the outside – because of their size

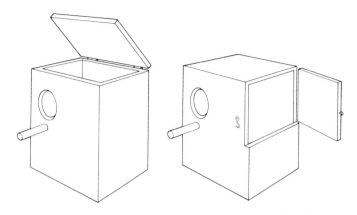

Nest boxes.

and the ease of inspection. You will need a hole in the cage lined up with the entrance hole in the box.

When the mating occurs, the hen crouches on the perch and forms her back into a hollow. The cock steps on to the hen's back, places one wing across her back, tucks his tail under her vent and mating takes place. Eggs are fertilised by the cock bird spraying sperm on to the hen's vent. Firmly fixed perches are essential if a mating is to be successful.

11 **Eggs and Chicks**

Once a hen has started to go into a nest box regularly, it will be about two or three weeks before the first egg is laid. The signs that a hen is going to lay are when the vent area becomes swollen, her tail pumps up and down and her droppings increase greatly in quantity and become wet. Once a hen has started laying she will lay an egg every other day. So after three days there will be two eggs, after five days there will be three eggs and so on. The number of eggs in a cockatiel's clutch ranges from about four to eight.

Unusually for parrot-like birds, both the cock and the hen cockatiel share the incubation of the eggs. Normally the hen sits from early evening until morning and the cock sits the rest of the time. It takes 21 days of sitting on the eggs (incubation) for them to hatch. Because the eggs have been laid every other day, the chicks will hatch every other day. Sometimes the pair does not begin sitting until the second or even third egg has been laid. Then, the first two or three chicks hatch on the same day – perhaps 25 days after the first egg was laid. Because of this staggered laying and hatching pattern, if incubation starts with the first egg, the first chick can be seven days old by the time the fourth chick hatches. When a

cockatiel egg is laid it is white in colour and you can see through the shell if the egg is held in front of a bright light. If the egg is not fertile it will remain like this. If the egg is fertile the yolk moves to the round end of the egg after three or four days of incubation. Then blood vessels can be seen as the chick begins to form. A couple of days later you can no longer see through the egg and it looks like a shiny white pebble. Do not be in too much of a hurry to judge that an egg is infertile, it may be that the pair has not started to incubate them.

Although you can open the nest box door once a day, to see that everything is going well, you should not interfere more than this. Cockatiels are very accommodating birds so it is easy to become over-confident as far as interference is concerned. A pair may object and leave their eggs. If a pair lets an egg get cold, during its 21 days incubation, the partly formed chick inside will die. The egg is then known as an addled egg and will change colour from a clear white and take on a grey tinge.

Some hours before an egg is due to hatch the chick can be heard calling, still inside the shell. When a chick is newly hatched it has a small 'horn' on its top beak. It is with this horn that it chips its way out of the shell. It pokes a small hole, turns a little, pokes again and goes on doing this until the end of the shell drops away, allowing the chick to leave the shell. If a chick does not succeed in getting out of the shell and dies in the attempt, it is known as 'dead-in-shell'.

Within a few hours of hatching, a chick will have been fed. As with sitting on the eggs, both cock and hen feed the chicks. First they eat the food and then bring it back up again to feed the chicks. This is called 'regurgitation'. If a chick's feet become caked in droppings, never try to remove the dirt by picking it off with your fingers. You could easily damage the partly formed feet. Instead, soak the feet in warm water and remove the droppings when they have become soft.

If you want to be able to identify each chick, so that pairings can be selected in later seasons, you may put closed, numbered aluminium rings on each chick at about ten days old or just before. You should check each day that the ring is clean and that there is no sawdust, seed or droppings trapped between the ring and the chick's leg. If you wish to identify an adult cockatiel, plastic split rings can be fitted at any age. It is important to use the correct size. Chicks leave the nest box when they are about five weeks old, though it can take from seven to ten days before every chick has left the nest. Within a week, chicks are usually capable of feeding themselves. To encourage this they can be offered millet sprays, greenfood and soft food. When you are sure that the chicks are feeding themselves they should be moved from the breeding enclosure. By this time the hen will have started laying another clutch of eggs. Two nests of eggs and chicks are enough if the chicks are to be strong and healthy. As long as there is a nest box available, cockatiels will carry on breeding until they lose their fitness, so to stop them breeding, remove the nest box.

12 Showing Cockatiels

If you are interested in cockatiels, other than as pets, a bird show is the place to go. Some shows are advertised in local newspapers, but to find out what clubs and shows are in your area you should buy *Cage and Aviary Birds*. This is a weekly paper which deals with all aspects of bird keeping and carries news of club meetings and shows.

Once you have located your local cage bird society you may choose to join. By comparing your cockatiels with other members' you will get some idea whether your birds are the type which can win prizes. The larger the show you go to, the wider the varieties of cockatiels you will see. You will notice that the birds are in good feather condition. Breeders go to a lot of trouble to make sure that their cockatiels are in perfect feather for a show. No judge will give a prize to a bird whose feathers are dirty and uneven.

There are sometimes classes put on specially for cockatiels in the Foreign Bird section of a show. If not, they have to compete with other parrot-like birds. With Foreign Birds it is usual for there to be only one classification. So that newcomers have to compete with more experienced exhibitors. An exception is made for juniors. The Junior section is for young

Page 57: Cinnamon

people, under the age of 16. If you are over 16 years of age you will start by showing your birds in open classes. With some other types of birds there are classes for Novices and Champions. Budgerigar exhibitors have three status levels to pass through before becoming Champions.

The open show season usually runs from July until December, though the majority of cage bird societies stage their events in the last three months of the year. If you decide to enter a show, you must obtain a suitable show cage. Cages are black and white and intended to look plain so that no cockatiel gains an advantage.

Club shows, staged just for club members, are usually easy going affairs, where you can turn up with your birds on the day to enter them. The Show Secretary will help you to enter them into the correct classes. Open Shows are more formal and your birds need to be entered in advance. When you find a show you would like to show at, send for a schedule. Ask an experienced breeder for help on which classes your birds should be entered in. Otherwise you may arrive at the show, after judging, to see 'W/C' written on your cage. This means 'wrong class' and that the bird has not been judged.

A few days before the show your cage labels will arrive through the post. Make sure that you stick the correct label to the correct cage before taking your cockatiels to the show hall. The schedule will show what time your birds need to be delivered to be in time for judging. It will also show what time the bird show

opens to the public, so that you can return to see if your birds have won. Better still, ask if you can help at the show, when you send in your entry form. If you do, you must be prepared for hard work, but the whole day will be spent with, and talking about birds and cockatiels in particular. What better way is there to spend a day?

I hope that after reading this book you still decide that you would like to keep a cockatiel – or even several cockatiels – and that the information you have read will help you to keep fit, happy and healthy pets.

Page 61: Pearl Pieds

The full range of
titles in the
LOVE YOUR PET SERIES is:-

Love Your Budgerigar
Love Your Canary
Love Your Cockatiel
Love Your Finches
Love Your Gerbil
Love Your Goldfish
Love Your Guinea Pig
Love Your Hamster
Love Your Kitten
Love Your Puppy
Love Your Rabbit
Love Your Tropical Fish